GOD'S CREATURES AT THE ZOO

GOD'S CREATURES AT THE ZOO

Wonderful Differences

by
Debra K. Stuckey

Illustrated by
Jules Edler

CONCORDIA®
Publishing House
St. Louis

3558 S. Jefferson Avenue, St. Louis, MO 63118-3968
Manufactured in the United States of America

Library of Congress Cataloging-in-Publication Data

Stuckey, Debra K., 1959-
God's creatures at the zoo.

Summary: Describes useful physical characteristics God gave some of the animals in the zoo.
1. Zoo animals—Religious aspects—Christianity—Juvenile literature. [1. Zoo animals] I. Edler, Jules, ill. II. Title.
BT746.S775 1986 231.7'65 85-17422
ISBN 0-570-04134-1

1 2 3 4 5 6 7 8 9 10 PP 95 94 93 92 91 90 89 88 87 86

To
Rachel and Joshua

Hooray! Grandma is taking me to the zoo today. We will see lots of different animals. All are special, because God made each one.

ZOO

The anteater has a silly, long nose.
He uses his nose to catch ants.
God made it that way.

The great big elephant has
a long nose, too. He uses it to
grab some grass to eat or
to take a shower.
God thought of
everything.

God gave the giraffe a sleek, long neck.He stretches his head way up high to eat the leaves at the top of the trees.

The monkey's long tail makes me giggle. Sometimes I wish I had one so that I could swing in the trees, too.

The ostrich is a bird, but he can't fly. So God taught him to run fast. He can run faster than my daddy!

The zebra looks like a horse with striped pj's. God gave him those stripes so that he could hide in the tall weeds.

Mr. Peacock spreads his pretty tail feathers. He is asking the lady peacocks, "Do you like me?" I do. He certainly is pretty.

The hippo looks fat and awkward on land. In the water he is a graceful swimmer. How did You do that, God?

There are a lot of people visiting the zoo today. God made each of them, too. We are all special to Him.

Thank You, God!

THE END